21st Century Junior Library

DISCOVER THE DEINOSUCHUS

Josh Gregory

Our Prehistoric World: Beyond Dinosaurs

Published in the United States of America by:

CHERRY LAKE PRESS
2395 South Huron Parkway, Suite 200, Ann Arbor, Michigan 48104
www.cherrylakepress.com

Reading Adviser: Beth Walker Gambro, MS, Ed., Reading Consultant, Yorkville, IL

Photo and Illustration Credits: © Racksuz/iStock.com, cover, title page; © Herschel Hoffmeyer/Shutterstock, cover (background), title page (background); © Racksuz/iStock.com, 5; © Björn Forenius/iStock.com, 5 (background); © GARY HINCKS/SCIENCE PHOTO LIBRARY, 6; © JULIUS T CSOTONYI/SCIENCE PHOTO LIBRARY, 7; © MARK P. WITTON/SCIENCE PHOTO LIBRARY, 8–9; Andrey Atuchin via Wikimedia Commons, 10; © VectorPlotnikoff/Shutterstock, 10; © James M. Chambers/Shutterstock, 11; © Savoul Pelister/Shutterstock, 12–13; © JOHN SIBBICK/SCIENCE PHOTO LIBRARY, 14; © Savoul Pelister/Shutterstock, 16–17; © Elenarts/Shutterstock, 18–19; Jonathan CutrerDerivative: User:MathKnight, CC BY 4.0 via Wikimedia Commons, 20

Cherry Lake Press is an imprint of Cherry Lake Publishing Group.

Library of Congress Cataloging-in-Publication Data has been filed and is available at catalog.loc.gov.

Cherry Lake Press would like to acknowledge the work of the Partnership for 21st Century Learning, a Network of Battelle for Kids. Please visit Battelle for Kids online for more information.

Printed in the United States of America

CHERRY LAKE PRESS

CONTENTS

WHAT WAS A DEINOSUCHUS?

Have you ever been near a crocodile or an alligator? These fearsome **reptiles** might remind you of dinosaurs. They have existed for many millions of years. Prehistoric crocodiles were even bigger than the ones today. One type was called the *Deinosuchus*. This name comes from the Greek words for "terrible crocodile."

Deinosuchus could weigh up to 10,000 pounds (4535.9 kilograms)!

Deinosuchus lived between 83 and 72 million years ago. It lived in what is now North America. Back then, the center of the **continent** was filled with water. *Deinosuchus* lived to the east and west of this watery area. It made its home in

This is what North America looked like when *Deinosuchus* lived. A modern map of the United States is shown laid on top of the area.

swamps, rivers, and coastal areas. Today, *Deinosuchus* is **extinct**, though no one is quite sure why. Scientists think that its environment changed. They think *Deinosuchus* wasn't able to **adapt** to the changes.

Think!

North America was very different when *Deinosuchus* lived. What do you think it was like back then?

WHAT DID A *DEINOSUCHUS* LOOK LIKE?

Deinosuchus looked a lot like the crocodiles and alligators that live today. It had a long body and short legs. Its long tail was strong and muscular. And it had a huge, powerful mouth. Its jaw was long and filled with dangerous teeth. A single *Deinosuchus* tooth was about the size of a banana!

Deinosuchus **had large teeth and a strong jaw to take down large predators.**

Even the dinosaurs living back then were not as big as *Deinosuchus*. *Deinosuchus* was about twice as heavy as a *Tyrannosaurus rex*. It could grow to be about 40 to 50 feet (12 to 15 meters) long. That's about the size of a school bus! The eastern *Deinosuchus* was slightly smaller than the one living in the west. But it was still huge!

This animal trainer does a live show to teach people about alligators.

The skin of *Deinosuchus* was hard and bony. It was covered in plates called **scutes** or **osteoderms**. These plates were like armor. They protected *Deinosuchus* from enemies. Today's crocodiles and alligators have them, too.

The scutes on a *Deinosuchus* didn't just act as armor. They helped propel *Deinosuchus* through the water.

Look!

You can see crocodiles and alligators at zoos or in videos online. Take a close look at their skin. Can you see the scutes?

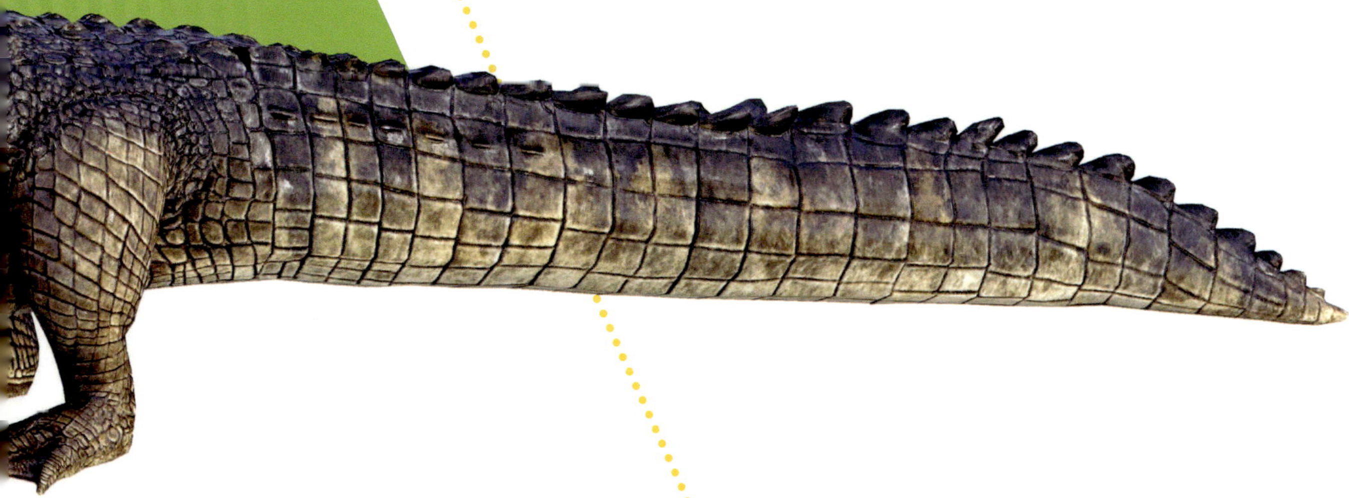

Deinosuchus likely attacked *Corythosaurus* when it came to get a drink.

HOW DID A DEINOSUCHUS LIVE?

Deinosuchus had eyes and nostrils on top of its long head. This feature let it breathe and see while hiding mostly underwater. Other animals walking past wouldn't be able to see it easily. *Deinosuchus* was patient. It waited for **prey** to get close. Then it quickly sprang out of the water and clamped down with its powerful jaws.

Almost any kind of animal living back then could be prey for *Deinosuchus*. It probably ate everything from dinosaurs to sea turtles. Its teeth could crush right through turtle shells. *Deinosuchus* swallowed its prey mostly whole. The only animals it couldn't eat were those too big to swallow!

Make a Guess!

If *Deinosuchus*'s teeth were not for chewing, what do you think they were for? Take a guess. Then ask a grown-up to help you find out if you were right.

Deinosuchus likely dragged its prey into the water to eat.

It took a long time for *Deinosuchus* to grow to its full size. Reaching adulthood probably took about 35 years. That's a lot longer than it took dinosaurs to grow up. While growing, *Deinosuchus* could be prey for big dinosaurs like tyrannosaurs. But once they were fully grown, they didn't have to worry much about **predators**.

Create!

What do you think it looked like when *Deinosuchus* fought a huge dinosaur? Try drawing a picture of one of these battles.

This *Deinosuchus* skull replica is on display in Big Bend National Park in Texas. *Deinosuchus* fossils have been found in the park.

Scientists have learned about *Deinosuchus* by studying **fossils**. Fossils of skulls and bones showed how big *Deinosuchus* was. Fossilized poop helped scientists learn what *Deinosuchus* ate. And fossil locations showed where *Deinosuchus* lived.

Want to see a *Deinosuchus* skeleton for yourself? You can find them in a number of museums. It's the closest you'll come to meeting this fierce animal in person!

Ask Questions!

Experts at museums love to share what they know. Ask them things you want to learn about *Deinosuchus*. You might be surprised at how much they know!

GLOSSARY

adapt **(uh-DAPT)** change in response to one's environment for comfort or survival

continent **(KAHN-tuh-nuhnt)** one of Earth's large landmasses

extinct **(ik-STINKT)** no longer found living anywhere on Earth

fossils **(FAH-suhlz)** remains or traces of plants, animals, and other living things that have been preserved as rocks

osteoderms **(AH-stee-oh-dermz)** hard, bony scales that covered *Deinosuchus* and other animals

predators **(PREH-duh-tuhrz)** animals that hunt other animals for food

prey **(PRAY)** animals that are hunted by other animals for food

reptiles **(REP-tielz)** cold-blooded animals that have backbones and reproduce by laying eggs

scutes **(SKOOTZ)** another word for the hard, bony scales that covered *Deinosuchus* and other animals

FIND OUT MORE

Books

Hofer, Charles. *Crocodile vs. Deinosuchus.* North Mankato, MN: Capstone Press, 2024.

Lundgren, Julie K. *Sea Monsters.* Ann Arbor, MI: Cherry Lake Publishing, 2026.

Websites

With an adult, learn more online with these suggested searches.

Western Australian Museum: Deinosuchus
Check out a map, a size comparison, and more.

PBS Dinosaur Train: Deinosuchus
Learn more about Deinosuchus with a fun cartoon.

INDEX

ABOUT THE AUTHOR

Josh Gregory is the author of more than 250 books for young readers, covering everything from video games and technology to dinosaurs and U.S. history. He lives in Chicago, Illinois.

ABOUT PALEOARTISTS

Paleoartists bring the prehistoric world to life! They work with scientists, paleontologists, museums, and their own research to recreate living things from long, long ago. **Mark Witton** is one paleoartist featured in this series. He has been studying prehistoric creatures for over 20 years! **Brian Engh** is another. He builds sculptures, too. He designs and builds whole exhibits. He started Living Relic Productions.